POWER
PARENTING

LIBERTY LEE

POWER PARENTING

TATE PUBLISHING
AND ENTERPRISES, LLC

Published by Tate Publishing & Enterprises, LLC
127 E. Trade Center Terrace | Mustang, Oklahoma 73064 USA
1.888.361.9473 | www.tatepublishing.com

Tate Publishing is committed to excellence in the publishing industry. The company reflects the philosophy established by the founders, based on Psalm 68:11,
"The Lord gave the word and great was the company of those who published it."

Book design copyright © 2016 by Tate Publishing, LLC. All rights reserved.
Cover design by Norlan Balazo
Interior design by Caypeeline Casas

Published in the United States of America

ISBN: 978-1-68352-353-6
1. Family & Relationships / Parenting / General
2. Religion / Christian Life / Family
16.05.25

I dedicate this book to my parents, who are the best parents in the whole world. May I live up to your legacy. I love you both more than you will ever know.

Thank you to the family and friends who have said, "You need to write a book," and to Jackie for helping me take that leap.

Thank you to Dr. Kathy, who has been a mentor and friend and helped me edit during crunch time. You are a dear friend and one of the smartest people I know.

And last but not least, thank you to my husband Ryan and our kids for putting up with a dirty house and piles of laundry as I tried to meet deadlines. Thank you for letting me tell our story and for your support and love.

CONTENTS

1   An Introduction 9

2   The Ground Rules 13

3   Follow Through 17

4   Only One Behavior at a Time 23

5   Making Deposits 27

6   Preference versus Principle 37

7   Life's not Fair 49

8   Be Prepared for the Tough Questions 53

9   If You Ever Get Arrested 55

10 The Law of Progressive Obedience 63

11 If You Get Pregnant or
if You Impregnate Someone Else 67

12 Have a Family Safe Word 71

13 Help for College 79

14 This Is for the Girls 85

Bibliography 89

1

AN INTRODUCTION

Another parenting book. Just what this world needs. I have never read a single one. Why not? I was in my thirties when I started having children and my logic was simple: if the average teenager can figure out how to get pregnant, how to birth the baby and how to raise it, then I certainly could too. Why read about it?

The first few months were easy enough and even the first couple years were not that hard, but then these kids began to talk and it was not long before I fully realized that they were far smarter than me. Then my theory changed to something like, how could the hospitals possibly send these little bundles of joy home without instructions, without a return policy, and certainly without screening me and my husband! No one asked me if I could read or write. No one asked me if I had a job or could cook a meal. Thank goodness! And the older these kids got, and like goonies they multiplied, things got really out of control. This is when I decided there should be a Mommy Training.

It should be some sort of combat style training. It would be different than traditional combat training where you maneuver through an obstacle while trying to kill the enemy. This would be an obstacle course where you try to maneuver through a mommy style course without killing the enemy.

Case in point: I'm cooking dinner. As I am beginning to serve up plates of food, one of my kids announces that the dog is throwing up on the rug in the playroom. I finish what I am doing and go to see the damages. It was a huge pile of grossness, so I head to the garage for a shovel. I begin shoveling the vomit and the kids abandon their dinner plates and begin asking questions,

"Why did Ranger throw up?"

"What did Ranger throw up?"

"Is that chicken?"

"Why did he throw up chicken?"

"Who fed him chicken?"

One kid goes into the room where my husband is and says, "Mom has a shovel in the house. Why does Mom have a shovel in the house?"

I hear Ryan quietly answer from the other room, which is kind of code for "adult hiding." It is the same logic a two year old uses when they don't like what is going on around them and cover their eyes believing that no one can see them. I let Ryan continue in this behavior because I know if I mention this, he will say, "Who did I buy the dog for? You. So you get to clean up his mess."

I ignore Ryan's adult hiding and the kids continue, "Why did Landry feed Ranger chicken?"

"Is that the same chicken we are having for dinner?"

"Why did he throw up?"

"If I eat that chicken, am I going to throw up?"

"Is Ranger sick?"

The only activity worse than having to clean up the vomit is being subjected to a full scale CIA like interrogation while cleaning it up. All it lacked was a little lightbulb hanging from the ceiling and threats of waterboarding.

So I propose a little combat readiness that should include but not be limited to the following.

- Full scale interrogation training: you have to be interrogated while performing terrible tasks.
- Kill zone training: only you are not allowed to harm, kill, or injure any parties including yourself.
- Psychological testing: including long term stress, sleep deprivation, and poor spousal behavior (just in case).
- Intellectual testing: just in case you want to be right when being interrogated (by the way, I care nothing about being right, I just want everyone to shut up!).
- Full scale torture training: because some days, this would come in handy.
- Training in all forms of weaponry: just in case you slip through the cracks of the screening process and

decide to go AWOL, then you have the skills to do it up right.

All teasing aside, why am I writing this book? Because I have been wildly successful with my own kids? No, not at all. Actually my kids are still quite young. I'm writing this because my own parents were like parenting geniuses or ninja warriors or Jedi knights. They were hugely successful in raising four children. (Gosh, now that I put that on paper, I worry that one of my brothers will get drunk and streak through the town square naked or something crazy.) Barring no major developments, my parents raised four decent and respectable adult children. Everyone went to college, everyone is employed, most are married and raising children, everyone attends church, and everyone serves in the community. No one did drugs, no one got arrested, no one is asking for a handout, and no one has run through the town square naked and drunk as of this writing.

We all still hang out, we vacation together, we text each other all the time. It's like my parents made the American dream family. And that my friends is why I am writing this book. I want to write down the cool things I experienced living with my parents so that you and I can make our own dream family, or at least have a better chance at it.

So here goes, let's enjoy the ride.

2

❧

THE GROUND RULES

Let's establish some ground rules: first and foremost, nothing replaces love. We all need it. And your kids deserve it. My parents made us feel so loved that to this day, as adult children, each and every one of us signs birthday cards or notes to our parents with "Your favorite." And just to show our confidence and utter lack of humility, we do not sign our name because naturally when we sign "Your favorite," it is obviously from *the favorite*, and they will know who that is. And no lie, each of us honestly believes it. How did my parents do this? I have no idea! How do four kids feel like they were loved more than the other three? Again, I don't know. But isn't that genius work by parents? I will tell you one thing's for sure: they somehow managed to love each of us and do something for each of us *individually* that made us feel super special.

Mom would sometimes lean over and whisper in my ear, "Do you know how special you are to me?"

"Do you know that I am so proud of how you worked through that problem with ______?"

"You are getting so good at ______."

"Do you have any idea how much I love you?"

And the best line ever, "You are my favorite because ______."

Now the magical thing about this is, SHE WAS WHISPERING THE SAME THING TO ALL OF US! MOM TOLD ALL OF US WE WERE HER FAVORITE! Being a Jedi knight, she naturally was very quiet about this. I did not pick up on it until much later in life. Was she lying? No, absolutely not. We each were and still are her favorite for different reasons. Now with Dad, I'm actually, really, really the only favorite. But don't tell the other kids.

This is so simple, but I want to say a little more about this. When do you as a parent bother to whisper in your kid's ear? It was completely random from my Mom. Sometimes it was after we had done something good, but more often it was when we were alone in the car, with an arm around us at church, when she tucked us in bed, during the middle of a TV show or over lunch, even sometimes after a punishment or lecture. Actually, the more random it was, the more meaning it had. We would be watching an evening TV show or having an intense conversation at lunch and out of the blue Mom would say, "Do you know how cool you are?"

I would think to myself, *Is she watching this TV show or is she thinking about me and my coolness?*

And suddenly I would feel more important than anything in the world.

3

FOLLOW THROUGH

Next, you have to follow through on your rules and your actions. I heard somewhere that the average parent warns their kid thirteen to twenty-one times before taking action. That's CRAZY! How can our kids take us seriously when we are that uncommitted to what we are telling them? Train yourself to follow through when the stakes are low so you will have the strength of character and resolve to follow through when the stakes are high. You will make mistakes and say stuff you don't mean.

You absolutely have to say *only* what you mean and *only* what you can follow through with. You are not always going to get this right. We had a little flub in this area just the other day when my middle child and I were out running errands. Stetson began bugging me about two months before Christmas, "Is Santa real?" After two months of avoiding his questionings I decided to set the record straight. It was a mistake on my part. Stetson has a sister a year older than him and a sister a year younger than him that still believe.

Against my better judgment, I revealed the truth. Stetson took it like a champ. But his immediate follow up question was, "What about the elf? Is the elf real?" (He was referring to our elf on the shelf).

I set him straight and he was far more devastated about the elf than Santa. In great disappointment he said, "Man, I really thought the elf was real. Are you sure?"

Before he finished that sentence I could see a light bulb going off in his head and he was excited and laughing, as he said, "I am going to touch the elf. IT WILL FREAK OUT THE GIRLS," referring to his sisters.

I couldn't help myself and laughed at his devious plan and said, "You better not do that."

I immediately called my husband and confessed my poor judgment and said, "Stetson wants to touch the elf and freak out the girls."

We both had a good laugh, but agreed that Stetson was about to ruin the magic of Christmas for both of his sisters.

After we arrived home some time later, Stetson bolted into the house. Ryan wisely grabbed him and we both escorted him directly to a back room. We closed the door and Ryan read him the riot act, threatened Stetson within an inch of his life, and ended with,

"If you touch the elf, I am taking all of your Christmas presents back!"

Stetson darted from the room promising never to touch the elf. I immediately folded my arms and did that very sexy look that every spouse loves of, "Way to go stupid!"

You know the look. You've done it before. Ryan shot back with the body language of, "No way, he won't do it. I got this."

This silent conversation took a matter of seconds and was not finished when we heard high pitched screams of terror from the living room.

"Stetson touched the elf! Stetson touched the elf!"

Being the mature parents we are, we both laughed at our son's antics for about half a second, then I self-righteously folded my arms and said to Ryan, "What are you going to do now?"

My high horse and I trotted into the kitchen and left Ryan alone to solve this little problem. And solve it, he did. Ryan made Stetson write Santa a letter apologizing for touching the elf and apologies were made to his sisters.

As parents, this was a great learning experience. Do not let emotions allow you to make comments you do not mean or have no intention of following through on. We have all screwed this up multiple times, but you have to minimize this and learn from your mistakes because your kids are smart. It only takes a few non-follow-throughs and they will no longer respect your word as truth, and why should they?

You will get better with practice and they will expect you to follow through on the big things because you have followed through on the little ones. If you say you are going to pull the car over, you have to do it. If you say they are grounded and prom is that weekend, they are grounded. If you take the car for a week, no matter how it inconveniences you, they may not have the car. If you take the cell phone for five days, don't give it back on day four.

This is one of the first parenting lessons found in the Bible. When Adam and Eve partook of the fruit, God did not say, "Well, ummm, I didn't really mean it. One more chance. Next time, you two are totally out of the garden."

I make light of this, but Our Heavenly Father followed through and how hard must that have been? The Lord knew the consequence was not only going to affect Adam and Eve but all of mankind.

For any crazy person reading this book, I am not advocating any form of child abuse or excessive punishments. I do not believe in striking your child in anger. We live in a state where corporal punishment is still legal and back when I was a kid, it was very socially acceptable. I had my butt spanked many times and am no worse off for it. But my parents never, never, never spanked in anger and certainly never left a mark on our bodies as a result of punishment. If you read nothing else in this book, read this: I remember doing some stupid stuff as a young kid and making my Mom so mad that I knew she might like to kill me. When she was really hot, she would say, "Go to your room! I am so mad right now that I cannot spank you."

Sometimes, it took a long time for her to cool off and in my room I remained, awaiting my punishment (which was worse than anything I had coming). After everything was calmed down, Mom followed through on my promised punishment, but I knew that she was spanking me because I deserved it, not because she was out of control. Never strike your child in anger! And if you are struggling with controlling your emotions and you cannot think of an appropriate punishment to fit the crime, don't panic. Tell the kid to go to their room and wait until you can gather your thoughts, confer with your spouse, phone a friend if you are a single parent. Just don't throw some crazy asinine punishment out in a fit of rage that you and your child know cannot possibly be followed through with.

4

ONLY ONE BEHAVIOR AT A TIME

This goes right along with what we've been talking about. My Mom taught me this as an adult when my three kids were driving me nuts. Let's talk "nuts" for a minute. My husband and I thought we were sooo smart to have three kids in just over three and a half years. Looking back we were sooo stupid. We were certifiably nuts and should have had our "sanity cards" revoked.

Naturally, we had the cutest, sweetest, most adorable little terrors I had ever seen. When they were respectively two, three, and four years old, I was sure that I had seen rabid animals behave better than my precious litter. I was about to take up drinking and smoking when my Mom said, "Focus on one behavior at a time."

She's so smart, it's like I was spawned from the "genius mother of all mothering," if there was such a thing.

My two oldest kids were struggling with being obedient, probably because I, always desiring to be above average, was warning them twenty-five times before I enforced what I was saying. Of course they were not quickly obedient. So I sat down with them and said, "We are going to work on obedience."

I told them the ground rules.

"I'll ask you to do something and I expect you to say, 'Yes, ma'am,' and do it. If you do not do it immediately, I will count to three and then The Enforcer comes out"—I then held up my wooden spatula—"no more warnings, no second chances."

I do not remember how they reacted to this, but I got my very supportive husband on board and we worked on this.

Keep in mind that a week is a long time from a kid's point of view and two weeks is an eternity in kid time. In about two weeks we had this obedience thing down much better than before. During this time I did not worry about lying, eating dirt from the plants, flushing objects down the commode, or peeing in the bathtub (which we still struggle with. What is it with that warm water?).

Of course you must praise your kids when they perform as you have asked. I am a big believer in praising as soon as they look like they are even thinking about doing the right thing. Be their cheerleader and biggest fan.

As the kids got older we added tangible rewards (not a lot older, remember we still pee in the tub occasionally). I read a fabulous book called *Daddy Dates* by Greg Wright. I very highly recommend this book. I won't spoil the book for you, but Greg takes his girls on dates as a way to spend quality one on one time with them and as a way to teach by example how a lady should be treated during courtship. A beautiful concept. Way to go Greg!

Allow me to further digress, I promise to bring all this full circle. In the past, my husband and I had tried all kinds of reward systems: pom-poms in a jar, coins from Chuck E. Cheese's, stickers, and all the usual things. We all lost interest after only a few days each time. You have to keep trying until you find something that works for your family. After reading Greg's book we started keeping tally marks on a whiteboard in our kitchen. At this time we were working very hard and specifically on controlling our emotions. When we caught one of the kids controlling their temper or not whining when they normally would or even correcting a whine, we gave them points. And we heaped on the praise. If they lost their temper, threw something in anger, cried unnecessarily, hit, etc., they lost points.

Once they earned twenty points, the board was cleared and the points could no longer be taken from the child because they had completed the goal. The reward: a date with the opposite gender parent. This has become so fun for us. At first, we did the traditional go to dinner thing, and that was okay. But at some point, Ryan got creative and started taking the girls for pedicures. (Guys, this was a super sexy thing for my man to do. The only reward better than me getting a pedicure is my husband taking my girls for princess pedicures. And FYI, they are cheaper than a regular pedicure.) Ryan had never had a pedicure before, but he quickly took to the time with his daughters, and who doesn't love to have their feet rubbed?

Stetson and I have done dinner, but we also do activities like go to an ice cream shop and play chess or run an errand specifically geared around his wants and grab buffalo wings, all that boy wants is buffalo wings. He's one hundred percent boy. Ladies, I have talked with my little man about what boys do on dates and this little six year old opens my door every time and without fail says, "Mom, wait right there." I'm in the driver's seat of course.

He runs around the car and opens the door for me. He is going to be a great catch some day.

We are rewarding and teaching all at the same time.

5

MAKING DEPOSITS

Speaking of rewards, make daily and consistent deposits into your child's emotional bank account. My parents did this in a less than conventional way. We ate out a lot. The time we spent waiting in line to get into restaurants, sitting at the table waiting for the food to be prepared, enjoying the meal together, sitting and chatting after the meal was complete were all huge deposits. We sat and spoke as friends. As kids, we opened up about what was going on at school.

Jedi knight parents do a magical feat during these times. They listen intently, act completely interested, and then ask the child, "What do you think about that?"

Oh I feel certain my parents had strong opinions that they were biting their tongues to not express, but instead they were teaching us to think for ourselves and talk through some of the crappy situations of the teenage years. I remember coming home and telling my parents that there were several girls that were pregnant at school (mind you, I was in junior high). My parents must have wanted to scream from the roof tops their advice, but instead I very distinctly remember what they said.

"And what do you think about this?"

"What do you think she is going to do to pay for their needs?"

"Is she still with the boy?"

"What is she going to do about school?"

Do you see what was going on here? My parents were showing genuine interest and instead of cramming their own beliefs and foresights down my throat, they were allowing me to develop my own beliefs and foresights under their tutelage. (I love the word *tutelage*. I think we need a new word *fartelage*.) Anyway, they were asking the questions that were making me think about the implications which in turn made me think, *I'm never going to do that.*

It was a win-win. Mom and Dad opened the lines of communication, did not pass judgment, helped me develop and think for myself, and we had a beautiful teenage experience together.

My kids are not teenagers and I do not have the luxury of eating out multiple times a week. My much disciplined husband keeps us on a budget and the "eating-out budget" would not foster relationships the way my parents did. So I had to come up with something else.

Several times a week, the kids and I take long walks together. Mind you, my kids are still young, but they can pretty easily click off a three-four mile walk with me. While this sounds very fabulous in theory, it is not always as beautiful in real life. We usually do not make it to the edge of the driveway before all three kids are talking loudly over top one another trying desperately to tell me something that is earth shattering to a six, seven, or eight year old. By the corner of our street, I am not really listening to anyone and am ready to pull my hair out, wondering why on earth I am doing this. But then I remind myself, "Someday, these kids are going to be teenagers and will not want to talk with you. Keep them talking now."

About half a mile into the walk, the clamoring for my sole attention has died down, even they are tired of the ruckus, and the rest of the walk is quite enjoyable.

If you are going to try this, I should warn you. Very typically the kids tell me things that are of no interest to any adult, but in becoming Jedi parents one must control his own emotions and listen intently as if Yoda himself were speaking. (Maybe I should confess right here that I have not actually seen *Star Wars*. Well, I saw an episode years and years ago, but I feel better confessing my ignorance to you now.) This is a test of endurance and you must patiently wade through all the trivial stuff and occasionally something really important will pop up. It's like panning for gold.

For instance, after many, many walks with nothing interesting surfacing with the kids, Landry, out of the blue, said, "There is a girl at my school who does not believe in God."

Ding ding ding! I just saw gold in the pan. Now let's turn on the ninja warrior parenting mode and very casually say, "Hmmm, interesting. What do you think about that?"

I quietly congratulate myself on my stealthy move.

Landry continues, "Well, she said her Moms won't let her believe in God."

I want to interrogate her about what she knows about having two Moms, but I try to keep my cool.

"Hmmm, what else did she say?"

Landry tears up and says, "Her Moms said that if she believes in God, they will take her back to the orphanage."

As you might imagine, my Mom radar was spinning like a top at that point. I was about to explode inside with things that I wanted to interject and say and teach and curse and all that. You feel me here, right? But I kept it together and quietly thanked God for Xanax.

"Landry, what do you think about that?"

My sweet baby girl got quiet. Tears welled up in her eyes and her face pinked up.

"I would ask to go back to the orphanage."

Oh my sweet child. All the emotions inside me stopped, and my soul was still, and I knew on this day, I had been taught. My child was wiser than any lecture I wanted to give. All that was left was to love and appreciate this moment—this precious little soul—and rejoice in her per- spective, which was beyond anything this mother could have taught on this day.

One more idea for teaching tools, behavior modification tools, whatever you want to call it: figure out what motivates your kid. Stetson is very motivated by money. Paris is very motivated by clothes and shoes. Being that two of my three kids like tangible rewards, we have a tangible system for all three kids to modify their reading behaviors. You will notice that this is not a good versus bad behavior. This is a,

"I want my kid to excel in reading behavior."

This applies to anything you want: piano, scouting, violin, getting homework done without moaning, household chores, etc.

I'm a reader. I value this and am trying desperately to impart this to my children. So I made charts that hang on the fridge. Each child has different reading goals in accordance with what I want to see from them. Landry, my oldest, has to read twenty minutes for school seven days a week and turn in a report for a grade. That's great, but I think she is old enough to be reading one hour a day. So I built her a chart that has blocks of time that equal one hour of reading for thirty days (that's the equivalent of reading one hour a day for a month). Stetson is still not one hundred percent reading on his own, and it is more difficult for him, so he has forty-five fifteen-minute blocks on his chart. Paris is at the very beginning stages of reading so her chart is not time based, it is book based. She has fifty books that she can either read or have read to her.

When a child completes their reading chart, which takes a little work on your part to keep up with, then they get thirty dollars. Holy, break the bank Batman! Do not panic. When we implemented this program we explained that each child was at a place in life where everyone had a good pair of athletic shoes, a good pair of school shoes, a good pair of church shoes, and a solid pair of cowboy boots. Their thirty dollars was for them to buy their own shoes from now on. The kids have completely bought into this.

Stetson, my biggest fighter against reading, jumped in whole heartedly and drove me a little nuts by wanting to read all the time. I would set him on the kitchen counter while I worked in the kitchen, turned on a timer, and he read. I was there to help with words he did not know and he got his minutes in while I got the dishwasher unloaded. Sometimes he read 30-45 minutes a day. It is great!

He was the first kid to earn thirty dollars, and I immediately took him out to buy a pair of shoes. He did not need a pair, but that's what he wanted and he earned it, so there you go. Can I just tell you that we went to no less than seven shoe stores and he liked absolutely nothing? After I was about ready to scream, we returned to the first shoe store and he bought an identical shoe to what he already owned, except in black. I wanted to have a conniption. But that would have ruined the moment, so I didn't.

As we walked back to the car and I was telling Stetson how proud I was of him for earning the money and buying his first pair of shoes all by himself, I noticed he was very quiet and his head was down. I stopped mid parking lot and said, "What's wrong?"

Tears began to flow and he said, "The money is all gone. I thought there would be some left."

This comment opened the door for us to talk about money and how expensive purchases are.

Moral of the story: I no longer have to ask my kids to read. Do they read every day? No! But do they read almost every day and with less nagging from Mom? Absolutely! And when Paris sees a pair of shoes that she cannot live without, she reads a lot more until the money is earned. And there is more to this little reward system!

First, we teach our kids about tithing. Each child pays ten percent to the church before they buy anything.

Second, they blew the money quickly at first but are now naturally learning how to save. Stetson was much wiser with his money the second time around and bought Scholastic books and saved the rest for his next pair of shoes. He doesn't need shoes right now, but he is preparing for the future need or desire. Landry used fourteen dollars to buy a toy from Scholastic books and it turned out to be cheap and was not as exciting as she had anticipated. The next time the Scholastic book orders came home, she made a better choice with her money. (Are you getting the idea that I do not buy Scholastic books either? I have nothing against Scholastic books, but I am against all the little fund raisers and nick-knacks that can nickel and dime me into poverty. I pay my taxes, that's what the schools get.) Anyway, our kids are learning the value of a dollar and we are letting them make mistakes with the money that they earn, but also teaching them the value of savings.

The third part of this system is that they are gaining self-worth and self-confidence. They love to tell grandparents how they bought a pair of shoes with their own money or to tell them what they are saving up for. They are learning to plan for the future and how to complete goals.

Power parenting—one system, three life lessons. Where did I learn this? From my ninja warrior parents. I remember they used to say, "We will pay twenty dollars for a pair of shoes. Anything above that, you must pay for yourself."

The end result: all my siblings pay a ten percent tithe, all save for future events, retirement, vacations, emergencies, etc., and all have huge tanks full of self-confidence and self-worth and are able to achieve individual and family goals. What more can a parent want for their children?

One more quick reward system: my sister has a board that has a dozen or so household chores on it. Under each chore is a clothes pin that holds one dollar. If a child wants to earn a little extra dough, they can choose to do a chore and the money is theirs. It teaches a lot of the same concepts we listed before. The important thing is to find something that fits your family goals, your children's needs, and follow through!

I have one huge concern with all these "systems" we have. Are you noticing that many are money based? It's true and I do not want my children to think that everything in this life is about money. But avoiding the money issue or not teaching it at all seems far more dangerous than using it as a reward.

6

PREFERENCE
VERSUS PRINCIPLE

Do you ever feel like you are hounding your kids to death? Grab a jacket, pick up your shoes, eat five bites of vegetables, don't lie, and brush your teeth. I feel like a broken record, a really bad broken record. I could provide directions on every single aspect of their lives. They need my help! Or at least it feels that way. A very good friend once said, "If it's a preference, let it go. If it is a principle, fight for it."

It is so simple and yet so wise. Kids have very few choices afforded them in their lives. Look at it from their perspective, we decide what time they go to bed, what time they get up, if they picked out acceptable clothing for school, what is for breakfast, what time we depart for school, what is in their lunch, which school they attend—it goes on and on and on. That does not count all the little "helps" we provide.

"Put on your seat belt, grab a book for reading time, brush your teeth, yes you have to have breakfast."

It is never ending. But you can help give your kids more freedom and yourself less fuss if you ask yourself, "Is this a preference? Or is this a principle?"

My oldest daughter does not want to eat breakfast before school. Do I prefer she eat? Yes. But is it a principle? Not really. She is a healthy eater. She isn't taking a medication that requires it. She's never passed out from low blood sugar. She doesn't have an eating disorder. She eats when she's hungry and stops when she's full. Why should we fight about it? So now I offer breakfast, she says no, and we move on. No fighting, no nagging, we leave the house happy.

Now when my son went through the lying phase, that was a principle—a big principle! So I was determined to fight my six year old to the death (being dramatic here) over something that is a must learn concept. You will tell the truth or you will suffer the wrath of Liberty every single time you lie. In case you are wondering who Liberty is, it's me, the author.

There is a popular family story that has been retold too many times about when I was in the first or second grade and my parents had taken us to a park called Sesame Place (it was a Sesame Street theme park). Afterward, I was playing with a friend and being not very socially adept, I bragged to her that my parents had taken us to this park. Not to be out done, my friend said, "Well, my parents took us to the circus."

I pressed her a little, decided she was lying and punched her, adding emphatically, "Don't you lie to me!"

I am still friends with this girl and her family, amazingly.

It has been thirty-five years since that incident, and my friend now lives up east. She was teaching a young Sunday school class about lying. She shared this little family story with her class and ended the lesson with, "So what is the moral of the story?"

To which they replied, "Don't lie to Liberty!"

It was not exactly what she was going for, but close enough.

I have to tell you another story. For this story you need to know that my husband is an engineer. He's a smart guy, sits behind a desk doing smart things that I don't understand.

I went to the school to meet with Stetson's teacher, she greeted me warmly, and we had the usual small talk. Then we sat down, and she said, "Stetson's a talker."

I whole heartedly agreed, replying, "Aaah, yes, but not everything he says is true so don't buy everything that falls out of his mouth."

She then asked with faked surprise, "You mean your husband did not parachute from a plane into your front yard?"

I slowly and somewhat shocked said, "Ummm, no. I don't think my husband has ever done that."

Seriously? Where does he come up with this stuff? While that story was super cool, it was not true and that is a principle. So it did not fly, any more than my husband parachutes. But just so you know, I did not discipline Stetson for this little embellishment because it gave me such a laugh. I encourage you to be a more mature parent than myself.

I have to share one more story on lying because our defeats are as important to learn from as our victories. One fine morning, we were all sitting in the car waiting for Stetson to join us. He was taking forever to pack his backpack. I honked the horn, waited, honked some more, and finally he got in the car. We were off to school. Later that day, I picked him up from school and he pulled from his backpack an entire box of double stuffed Oreos. I said, "Who put those in your back pack?"

He said, "I don't know. I didn't."

"Stetson! Do not lie, just tell me who put them in there."

He holds his ground. "Mom, I didn't do it. Maybe Dad did."

I had a medical procedure that morning and was not at the top of my parenting game. I was not in the mood to sort this out and was hoping time would help.

"Go to your room."

After about ten minutes he came out.

"Mom, I did not lie. I did not put the cookies in my backpack."

"Stetson go to your room."

He began to cry and went back to his room.

Thankfully, Ryan came home early on this day. I pulled Stetson into the kitchen with Ryan, relayed the events of the afternoon and Ryan offered to sort it out.

"Stetson, you have not lied to me, so there is no punishment. Now tell me what's going on."

Stetson stuck to his guns.

Paris wandered into the room. I have no idea what so inspired Ryan, but he tabled the issue and scooped Paris up into his arms. They played and cuddled and laughed and giggled until Ryan said to her, "Did you put anything into Stetson's backpack today?"

She said with confidence and not an ounce of shame, "Yes."

Ryan said, "Why didn't you tell Mommy it was you that put the Oreos in the backpack?"

Again, with confidence and justification in her voice, she said simply, "She didn't ask me."

I think we can all agree, if nothing else, Paris will be street smart.

I want you to know that I apologized to Stetson over and over. He generously agreed to forgive me and earned two points for telling the truth even when being punished for lying. He was reminded that life is sometimes not fair, even when he does everything right.

Additionally, I heard Ryan pull Stetson aside and provide a further lesson on this situation two days later. He explained that Stetson had a history of lying and how this was like the boy who cried wolf. You can see where this is going, so I won't belabor the point, but for the dads who might be reading this, it is excellent to participate in power parenting. The only thing better than one good parent is two good parents.

There is a little more to this story. The morning after the Oreo cookie caper, I was doing morning "stuff" and saw the Oreo cookie box on the counter. I couldn't resist. I planted it in Stetson's backpack. I neatly placed the backpack on the table but intentionally left some items out so he would have to finish packing things up himself. Stetson flipped open his back pack and saw the Oreos in there. His eyes turned to saucers and his jaw hit the floor. He started stammering, "Mom, I didn't. Who? I didn't."

I faked anger. "Stetson!"

The stammering never stopped.

"I promise. Who? I didn't."

I quickly let him off the hook and you could just see the air let out of his little chest as he breathed a sigh of relief. I had a good laugh, but I'm not sure he cared for the prank. And just think, you are taking parenting advice from me! Disclaimer: I am permanently ineligible to apply for Mother of the Year and prove it at least once a week.

Back to the principles and preferences, two of my three children will not wear warm clothes even on the coldest of days. This is really tough for me to admit, but it's a preference. They prefer short sleeves no matter the weather, and last year, on a snow day when the schools were closed due to inclement weather, Paris could be found sporting her swim suit as she enjoyed a day off.

I bite my tongue until it bleeds as I watch them crawl from the car, looking like young bulls breathing steam from their nostrils because the air is so cold. They are free to choose and although it pains me to no end, it is not actually wrong. I worry that schoolteachers will think bad of me or someone at Walmart will judge me an irresponsible parent. To make me feel only slightly better, when winter approaches, I send a note to school teachers saying, "Yes, my child has warm clothes and coats and all proper winter attire, but they generally choose not to wear it. Please do not call CPS." Then I explain my logic of preferences versus principles. Yep, I'm a freak. And contrary to old wives' tales, they won't get sick from cold weather; they get sick from viruses and bacteria. And what if they did get sick because their immune systems were compromised from fighting frost bite? In that case, they get to stay home with Mom for a snuggle day. We all win!

And just as an aside note, I use this little trick with my spouse too. When he does something that annoys me to no end, I try to stop and ask myself, "Preference? Or principle?"

You would be surprised, we spend a lot of time fighting over our own personal preferences with our kids and our spouses. Who needs that?

Case in point: Sunscreen. My very beautiful and very bald husband refuses to put sunscreen on until after he is three colors of lobster red. He says, "I'm tanning."

Ryan honesty believes this.

"Whatever, dude, you have no melanin."

I fought him on this until I finally came to my senses. Is sunscreen a preference or a principle? L'Oréal put the first sunscreen on the market in 1936. It's been around awhile, we know it to be of benefit to our skin, but it's not the Ten Commandments. It is a preference! I have to tell myself this over and over as I watch his skin blister and peel. Long ago, it occurred to me that my husband probably did far more damage in the thirty years before he met me than he has done in the last twelve years being married to me. After too many silly arguments about wearing hats and sunscreen, I finally made him a deal.

I said, "I am interested in your health and well being, but I promise to never hound you about sunscreen again if you will go get your skin checked once a year by a dermatologist."

Agreement made and now we don't argue…about this. It's one less point of contention and one more way to make memories at the beach and the lake and at soccer games and in the yard.

These are quite easy examples, but sometimes principles can be tough. Take church for example. Is church attendance a preference or a principle? Stop reading and take a minute to decide for yourself. You can't be wonky on this. Pick a hard line.

So what did you decide? Now that you've decided, can you please send me your vote because my husband and I cannot agree on this one. Ryan is very much a letter of the law kind of guy. He never, never, never misses church. What a blessing, right ladies? I struck gold on this guy.

But being that there is resistance in all things, I have desperately tried to convince Ryan that a Sunday off once or twice a year is okay. My argument being, "I'm in this for the long haul, I have to pace myself. You don't want me to get translated do you?"

To which he reassures me that I'm in no danger of being translated and to get in the car before we are late for the opening hymn.

So what do we do with our kids? Right now, they are too young to decide for themselves. Ryan says, "As long as you live in my house, you go to church every Sunday with me."

And that is that. Not a bad stance.

I was raised that you attended church most every Sunday, but it could be any church. As long as you were searching for something higher, that was acceptable. Of course my parents had their feet firmly planted in their own religion by the time us kids were around, but as converts to the faith, they appreciated the road of diligently searching.

Another little Jedi warrior tactic my parents employed for Sundays was a dinner that rivaled Thanksgiving every single Sunday! This motivated us on many fronts. The number 1 rule: if you went to church you got dinner. The number 2 rule: if you did not go to church, you had to prepare the dinner. And the number 3 rule: any of your friends who attended church on Sunday (any church) got to come eat with us. You see, the Jedi knight tactic, really it was more of a Pavlov-like move. They bribed us with food! And our friends too! Not only did they have a positive impact on us, they did on our buddies too. Our friends would say, "Hey, I'm going to church with my parents. See ya afterward for dinner."

This worked great for many years, but by the time we reached college, a funny thing happened. We had a friend who played wheelchair basketball for the local college. He came for Sunday dinner and we sent him home with left overs. Next time he came, he brought a buddy. Both boys went back to the college dorms with left overs. The other wheelchair basketball team members got wind of this and said, "Where is all this good food coming from?"

Before we knew it, there were six and seven wheelchairs crowding my parents' home for Sunday dinners. And this went on for a long time.

Think of the influence on people my parents were having by saying, "If you go to church, any church, you can come eat Sunday dinner here any time."

Our volleyball teams, basketball teams, kids from church, kids from school, all were encouraged by this large effort on my parents' part. It is no small deal to feed that many people from a modest home on a middle class income for years at a time.

So back to the original question: is church attendance a principle or a preference? I know that the basic Ten

Commandments say very explicitly, "Keep the Sabbath day holy." However you choose to interpret this—it's a principle.

7

LIFE'S NOT FAIR

When I was in junior high, I somehow was elected to be the face of a fund-raiser. I have absolutely no idea how this came about. I would not say I was a popular kid and so maybe this was just a joke, but I was essentially nominated to the position of "best class beggar." Yeah, it's not really something to be proud of, even in junior high.

There was a girl and a boy nominated from each grade and our goal was to raise money for some charity. Being a somewhat competitive person, I poured my heart and soul into this. I really wanted to crush the popular kids from the other grades. I do not remember many details about this, but I recall with great clarity that I got wind of the results—I had won. That is until the parents of the ninth grade contestant helped with the final tally and threw in a few extra bucks to put their daughter on top.

I remember being a little ticked off but do not remember how I relayed this to my parents. I can promise you this, if I came home upset or feeling cheated, my mom would have let me wallow in it for a very short period of time and then would say, "Life sucks, then you die."

As far as I know, my Mom coined this phrase. It was her way of saying, "Life's not fair, get over it." This is such a great lesson and I tell my kids all the time, "Life's not fair. It never has been and never will be. The best place to learn that is right here from me."

It's like a little poem. If you get a rhythm going, it even rhymes. Do not always jump in and save your kids from injustices. The lessons learned from injustices are as important as the victories. But if you always swoop in and save them, then they will come to expect it and will not learn what you and I already know so well. Life truly is not fair. So get over it! You can do everything right and by the book and still get crapped on. Learn to take it with a shovel and a smile and move on. This sounds like I'm an advocate of hands off parenting. Not really. I'm more a proponent of hands on when it is really important and hands off when it doesn't matter. The trick is figuring out which is which.

One of the best lines in the song "100 Years" by Five for Fighting sings, "I'm fifteen for a moment, caught in between ten and twenty."

This is a very profound vocal. Think about it: at ten years old you are completely and totally dependent on your parents for everything: food, shelter, love, transportation, clothes, absolutely everything. And we are still making a lot of their decisions for them. On the other hand, at twenty years old, you can be completely independent in every aspect of your life. But during that time between ten and twenty, kids are trying desperately to break into independence while still remaining dependent. It is a tough balance, and often, they are inconsistent in their behavior and so are we as parents. We throw them a bone of freedom in one aspect and then keep them reeled into our safe arms in many others. We tell them they are old enough to pick out their own clothes, maybe launder them or iron them and in the next breath, we screech, "You will not leave the house wearing that! We are going to church, not the club!"

And maybe they shouldn't leave the house as they are dressed, but can you see why the teenage years are just as difficult for them as they are for the parents?

We need to build a base on the important things so that as we relinquish freedoms and as they spread their proverbial wings, we can have a good experience together. This will build trust. This will build good decision making. And let's face it, all we really want is for our kids to make good choices. And the more they can do that without us present, the more safe and successful they will be.

This takes communication. This takes thought. This takes planning. Yes, it is going to be painful! It should be, but it is less painful than the alternative. Think of it as investing. I am not going to lie, several times when I've been parenting kids and my stamina is shot, I mutter under my breath, "I'm doing this now so I do not have to visit them in prison later."

Yes, I actually say these words to myself, sometimes out loud when I think I do not have the strength to go the extra parenting mile.

8

❧

BE PREPARED
FOR THE TOUGH QUESTIONS

So let's begin building the base, the foundation of good decision making. Remember those family dinners my parents had? This is a great time to slip these little conversations right in.

I'm no pediatrician or counselor or anything, but in my nonprofessional opinion, I think these conversations are best had while you are still the primary influence in your child's life, which means before age twelve, maybe even before age ten. A good friend once said, "It takes forever to get them to twelve, and then they are gone."

Let's have these conversations before they are gone, so to speak.

One of my all-time favorite movies is *42*, the Jackie Robinson story. If you don't know who Jackie Robinson is, he was the first African American to play major league baseball. It's a great story, you should check it out.

Jackie Robinson was invited to be part of the Brooklyn Dodgers. A young reporter assigned to Robinson was frustrated because Robinson refused to answer questions or give an interview. The very wise reporter asked Robinson to consider how,

"These are just the first of many tough questions to come, and they aren't going to get any easier."

He further reasoned with him.

"You know how you'd like to see the pitch come slowly toward you? Well, maybe you'd like to see those questions come slowly, too."

As a parent it would be advantageous to already have the answer to many of the hard questions long before they are asked. It helps the "pitch come slowly," and you can then knock it out of the park with confidence. I have flubbed many questions with my kids because I got blindsided.

9

IF YOU EVER GET ARRESTED

The odds of your kids getting arrested are probably pretty low. But preparing for this situation establishes a precedent in your child. It gets the wheels turning in their head and them thinking. And I promise this will play to your advantage.

I remember my Jedi knight parents having this conversation with us kids. It went something like this. "If you ever get arrested, do not call us because we will not bail you out."

This was their decision, their position, and their right as parents. They were so good at following through that we knew as kids, and later as young adults, that if we got involved in something bad and got caught, we were not calling Mom and Dad because they firmly believed,

"If you are smart enough to get yourself into trouble, then you better be smart enough to get yourself out."

This sounds easy enough, but you and your spouse need to be completely together on this because when or if you ever get that phone call that your kid is in the pokey, it is not going to be easy to let them sit there. I'm immediately concerned that my son is now some other dude's newest girlfriend and I am going to have nightmares about this until I know he is safe.

Why is it we think our kids are less safe in jail than they are on the streets? As if we've been to jail and know.

We never got arrested, but we did get in smaller forms of trouble with the law and guess what? We never called Mom and Dad!

On two separate occasions my baby brother got speeding tickets, and at that time, he was not in a position to pay. He was out of state, living lean, and he knew he had to solve the problem himself. He called me. I wired him money and we never told Mom and Dad. See how that works? Because the law had been laid down early, we had consciously or subconsciously figured out how to solve our own issues as young adults. What a weight and burden off my parents. You say, "Well, speeding tickets are nothing."

You are right, but multiply one or two speeding tickets by four kids and then you are mortgaging the house.

There was one time that my parents broke their own rule about bailing kids out of jail and to this day we have not let them forget it. My parents and sister were helping some kid find God. He showed an interest in religion, started going to church, and started cleaning up his life. One morning we kids woke up. Mind you, my sister and I were in our early

twenties living at home—working and going to college—
while our brothers were probably in their late teens. So my
parents sat us down and started this confessional.

"Last night, after y'all went to bed, we got a phone call
from the jail and Rex had been arrested for ———. We went
down to the jail and bailed him out."

We almost rioted!

"You did what?"

"You said you would never come get us—your own kids!"

To which they firmly reassured us, "And we still will *not*
come get you. That has not changed."

We were incensed and mutiny was the call of the hour.

"This is not fair!"

Why were we up in arms? I mean seriously, not one
of us was ever near any situation where we might be in
the slightest of trouble, but we wanted to be bailed out.
It made almost no sense, but we were incensed—literally.
Their word, their very bond, had been broken and we were
not going to let it go. I distinctly remember one of the kids
saying, "You said you would never come bail us out! Why
would you possibly bail him out? He's not even your kid!"

To which my parents said, "We never told Rex we
wouldn't bail him out."

And that was that. And to this day, we have not let Mom
and Dad live this one down. As a follow-up, I think Rex did
keep working on cleaning up his life and eventually mar-

ried and had kids. So I guess it worked out for the best, but we don't care. We just want to be bailed out!

Before we move to the next question, I want to tell you about my daughter in the second grade. (Yep, we just skipped from jail to second grade and I am going to link them together. Stick with me here.) Every month since kindergarten our school requires the kids to memorize a selected poem and recite it by memory for a grade. By the second grade Landry was getting really sick of this and started giving me attitude, bemoaning the work, and even crying about having to memorize. After a couple of poems I realized we were establishing a horrible behavioral pattern. She whined and cried, I crammed the poem down her throat, and we got a good grade. All this was at the expense of driving a wedge in our homework relationship, which has many, many more years to come. So I made a change.

The next poem that came home, I was ready with my ninja warrior parenting intervention.

Each evening I offered to help Landry with her poem. She shirked the duties but instead of fighting with her, I simply said, "Okay, we won't work on it, but the day is going to come and I cannot help you."

Two weeks of this passed and finally the day of truth loomed. The night before, I e-mailed Landry's teacher and warned her that Landry did not know her poem. Being that Landry is very shy and I knew standing in front of the class without knowing her poem might be a little more than what I was going for, I asked that the teacher handle it privately if she felt that was appropriate. I also asked that Landry get what she had coming because the teacher was super nice and I was afraid she might take pity on my kid.

The morning came and I was feeling all strong and like a Ninja Warrior Mom. Then the ride to school came. I noticed Landry had shrunk down in her seat, her complexion red, and tears streaming down her face. All the sudden, I was nervous for her and my heart was completely crushed. I tried to remain strong and delivered her to school as if nothing was wrong, but my life was over! I just knew I had made the wrong decision. I called my mom who tried to buoy me up and reassure me. I only felt slightly better.

I was a mess all day. I prayed, I didn't eat, I drank too many Dr Peppers. I was nervous and sad, second guessing and thinking I was such a jerk for a mother. I e-mailed the teacher to keep me posted on how it went. I'm sure she thought I was a freak. Only after my guts had turned on me and I was considering checking myself into a behavioral unit, did Ms. Thomas e-mail me with an update.

Ms. Thomas kindly reported that Landry had been called to her desk to recite the poem. I'm sure Landry was in about the same state as I had dropped her off to the school, red faced with tears. (Still imagining this today breaks my heart in two. I really should seek counseling.)

Ms. Thomas said, "Landry, do you know your poem?"

Landry said, "No."

Ms. Thomas allowed Landry to recite what little she had learned since that morning. Somehow Landry had managed to learn enough to make a thirty. Not bad. But Ms. Thomas was very wise and held Landry fully accountable. She e-mailed me and said, "Landry will spend recess walking the track memorizing her poem until she can recite it to me, but the grade sticks."

I loved that!

Lesson learned. To this day, we have no problem memorizing poems ahead of time and I actually do not have to help her as much. We both suffered long and hard that day, but we are better people for it. Her behavior improved immediately and has lasted.

Point being, if I can be such a boob and almost break down over my child not knowing her poem in second grade which had absolutely no bearing on her life or safety, how hard is it going to be when she calls from jail? It will kill me! And it will kill you too. We must practice while the stakes are low and build up our resolve. I imagined horrible things happening to my child, like her standing embarrassed and humiliated in front of the class, and suddenly I was no ninja warrior mom—I was a crazed maniac who wanted to spare her baby the natural consequences of her actions. If you love your child, you will feel the exact same as I did, and the level of love and emotion will be completely overwhelming. I know!

In retrospect, I am so glad I stuck to my guns, but no lie, it was horrible! A few hours of suffering has paid great dividends for both of us. And you will notice that my spouse supported this. He did not undermine my parenting by sneaking Landry into a closed room and cramming the poem down her throat. Bless this man. I am sure it is no walk in the park being married to me.

There is no way to predict what might happen in our lives, but we can plan and resolve to try to do what is best. We must practice and look—yes, I said look—for opportunities to practice. We are exercising our parenting muscles so we can be strong when it really does count.

10

THE LAW
OF PROGRESSIVE OBEDIENCE

I start teaching this principle as soon as kids can buckle their own seat belts. We have a car with three rows and everyone wants to sit on the middle row that contains the captain's chairs. Ugh! Does this fight ever end? Any Mom knows exactly what I'm talking about. There is always a coveted seat, whether it is by the door or toward the front or whatever. It's just another good reason for kids to fight.

I have explained to my kids that they all sit on the back bench until they can show one hundred percent responsibility. What does that responsibility include? I explain to them that their only responsibility is to put on their seat belts without being asked and to leave them on! On that back row the windows do not go up and down, there are no door handles, and there are no buttons. It's kind of boring. But once they can be one hundred percent responsible, one hundred percent obedient without being asked, they can move up to the middle row of seats.

Now this is exciting. They have more freedom, but they also have more rules. There are doors that they must not open while the car is moving. There are windows that they cannot roll up and down at random, and they still have to wear a seat belt. But they can now control the temperature of the air, they can open and close the overhead movie screen, and they can ask to open and close windows and doors. As they are obedient, they gain more freedoms.

The next exciting goal is to sit in the front seat someday where there are lots of buttons to the radio, heated seats, reclining chairs, DVD player, volume, and all sorts of things. They must master the captain chairs in the back before they can gain this next level of freedom. Of course, we must also follow the law of the land and not sit up front until the law allows.

The ultimate goal is to get to drive the car. To achieve this, we must show the ultimate obedience to get the ultimate freedom. One must master the art of self-control, take a class on obeying laws of the road, show responsibility with seat belts, and so much more. But you see where this is going. Freedoms are gained through obedience and as the freedom progresses, so do the laws of obedience. If the laws are not followed, privileges are taken away. This teaches children exactly how the world around them works. What happens if you get a DWI? Or if you get too many speeding tickets? There are penalties. You can ultimately lose the right to drive a car.

When we were kids, my parents would let us stay out with friends as long as we were honest about where we were going, who we were with, and what we were doing. I could go anywhere and stay out as long as I wanted. When I left one location to move to another, I called my parents to tell them. If we changed plans, I let my parents know. But if I ever abused this or my parents couldn't reach me, all freedoms were revoked and I had to start over in proving my willingness to be obedient. My parents made that such a process, it was just easier to do what was right.

11

IF YOU GET PREGNANT OR IF YOU IMPREGNATE SOMEONE ELSE

I'm not going to lie, there is nothing funny about this topic. Being a grandparent is among our fondest dreams and our worst fears. (1) Who wants to be that old? Not me! (2) Who wants to spoil a kid and then send them home? Me! Grandkids are God's little reward for not killing our own children.

I remember "the talk" from my parents. First, I got "the talk" from a playmate when I was six or seven years old at most. She was kind enough to "show me" using Ken and Barbie while my mom was socializing in the other room. Mind you, this was a girl from church, and her babysitter—also from church—was kind enough to have told her how this all works. So much for the church kids being the good ones. And she told me a little wrong. Let's just say her physiology was a smidge off.

I went home and asked my mom about these things and she set me straight. It was so gross that I cried. Because crying makes it less gross? I don't know why I cried. I just did. When Landry was about to turn eight, we decided that we would give her "the talk." Ryan played his "I'm-an-awesome-dad card" and said he wanted to be there when I told her. We went into the bedroom and closed the door. I did most of the talking. I thought it would be easy. I'm very comfortable talking about all kinds of subjects, but this seemed rocky in its presentation, even Ryan tried to jump in and help. Landry took it well, did not cry, and said she did not have any questions. Landry left the room and Ryan said, "That was terrible. You should have practiced."

I hate to admit it, but he was right. Oh well, first kids are for practicing on, by the time Paris gets "the talk," I'll be a pro.

When I entered sixth grade, I knew people were "doing it" or at least claiming to be. By ninth grade, I knew ten girls who had become pregnant. About sixth or seventh grade my parents built on the sex talk with, "This is what we believe."

They gave their stance on morals, and obviously, they gave this with the sex talk, but this was more specific. They said, "If you become pregnant before the age of eighteen, you will give the child up for adoption. If you become pregnant after eighteen, the choice is yours, but you will not live here. We are not raising your children." It was not complex, it was not a threat; it was just the expectation. This may not be a popular position, but it is my belief that "children are entitled to birth within the bounds of matrimony, and to be reared by a father and a mother who honor marital vows with complete fidelity."

Some people do not embrace a strong moral obligation until after they are married or until they have children or until they find God or after they have an STD flare up, which is kind of like finding God but in a bad way. Whatever motivates you. What do you tell your kids then? The truth! You can say, "This is what we believe. We have not always had the benefit of acting as responsibly, but we would like for you to. We believe this to be the best way because _______________. We wish we had not done these things _______________, and we wish we had done them this way _______________."

No, I am not going to give you a cheat sheet of answers.

I cannot tell you what to believe, you must decide where your convictions lie and pass them along to your children. You do not have to be perfect in everything to set an example for your kids. We are all evolving and we want better for our kids than we ever had, and that includes standards of greatness. Raise the bar in your home. Do not say, "Well, I did not do it, so how can I ask that of them?"

That's crap! That's a cop out! Sure you can. You openly admit where you have been wrong, tell them how you have corrected and mended your ways, and bless them with higher standards than you had.

And don't forget to have that little chat about, "If you get pregnant or impregnate someone else, then—"
It's important!

12

HAVE A FAMILY SAFE WORD

If you feel unsafe or just need an out, I will come get you, no questions asked.

Reba McEntire sings a great song called "What Do You Say."

A part of the lyric sings,

> Seventeen years old
> She was out with her friends
> They started drinking at some party
> Till she was three sheets to the wind
> Her momma always told her she could call no
> matter what
> She was crying on the front steps
> When her mom showed up
> So what do you say in a moment like this
> When you can't find the words to tell it like it is
> Just bite your tongue and let your heart lead the way
> Let's get out of here
> Oh what do you say.

Kids are going to do stupid things. No matter how good a parent you are, there is the chance that they will get in a bad spot and need you, really need you. My parents always encouraged us to prevent getting into bad situations in the first place, but if we found ourselves in a spot, we always knew that we could call and Mom and Dad would come get us (except for the jail thing), no questions asked.

My sister was very, very social. She played on very competitive volleyball teams, which meant lots of parties with the girls and boys and alcohol or worse. My parents were concerned, but because my sister had been responsible and shown good judgment, they allowed her to attend parties. Very often alcohol was involved, but my sister would go and encourage as many girls as possible to do the right thing and leave with her. My parents would get a phone call at all hours of the night.

"Can you come get me and a few other girls?"

No matter the inconvenience, the hour, their own fatigue, our parents would fire up the car and go pick her up and usually a car load of girls. After several of these pickup runs, I remember my parents saying to my sister, "Why are you going? You know we are just going to have to come get you?"

She said, "I have to go help some of these girls get out of there."

Not everyone has parents who will come get them. Very often, the police were called to these parties, but my sister never stayed that long.

Thankfully, this was about the extent of things for our little family. But it is not uncommon for a girl to get on a date and decide she is no longer safe or for a boy to be out with the guys and all the sudden realize things are getting out of control. Let's be for real, the teenage brain is not fully developed and they do not always see things coming like an adult brain. We should not hold this against them but should give them an out.

Develop a code word, something simple, easy, and distinct.

My sister played on a volleyball team and wore the bun hugger shorts, things that looked like swim suit bottoms. For whatever reason, they developed a system of code words to tell each other things about their butts. (Yes, this is stupid, just keep reading.) If someone's underwear had crept outside the bounds of the shorts and was showing, they would say, "Elvis lives. Right side."

The next one I never understood, but they would say, "Your dog is dead"—which somehow translated to, "Your butt is sweating and I can see it."

(As if this had any bearing on anything or the player could do anything about it.)

So you need a code word or phrase. Have fun with this and make it easy to remember.

"Hawks circling the carcass."

"Mary Poppins is real."

"The dog is dead."

"Circling the drain."

"Friendly fire."

"Elvis lives."

"Redskins beating Cowboys."

The Redskins should never beat the Cowboys, so it is an obvious sign that something is imminently wrong when someone uses that phrase.

"Alaska is on fire."

Pick something that means something to you and your family and use the phrase when you are in distress. This will allow your kids to remember the phrase and you too. When the toilet is overflowing, yell, "Elvis lives! Elvis lives!" And hope someone comes running to help.

Laugh at your kids when they holler, "Friendly fire! Friendly fire!" when they are needing your immediate help on homework. Make it fun so that when the day comes and your kid needs out and immediate safety, they can use your code phrase without outing themselves to their date or their friends or anyone else. They can text it to you without having to explain. They can say it before hanging up from a phone call. It makes it easy.

You also need to establish a "trouble free zone." You should have one of these anyway but formally create a situation where your kid can tell you anything and will not get in trouble within the limits of the law. Underage drinking does not count, while intentionally harming another person or their property is inexcusable *always*!

Every few years or so, usually around Christmas or a holiday, we four kids would be sitting around and have what we called "confession." That is when we told Mom and Dad about the stupid things we did, usually years ago and well outside the statute of limitations, so we all had a good laugh about it—well, we kids laughed, anyway. When we told Mom and Dad that we had put our youngest brother in the dryer and turned it on, Mom freaked out. We were like, "What? Don't freak out, it was years ago, and we put pillows around him so he wouldn't get hurt, and we left the dryer door open so he wouldn't die!"

My parents said, "The dryer doesn't run with the door open."

To which we replied, "We put one kid on top of the dryer to turn it on, and one held the trip button near the door so the dryer thought the door was closed. It works when you do it that way."

They did not like that anymore than the time we took our little brother outside to the frozen over swimming pool and made him see how far he could walk across it. Not very far it turns out. Mom and Dad just shrink into the couch when holiday confessionals come around.

Anyway, create a Trouble Free Zone where your children can use your special phrase and know that they can come home without getting into trouble. Start this very young.

When I was in elementary school, I did not particularly care to spend the night at other people's homes. So my parents let me stay until bed time and then they came and got me. I hung out with very good girls, and they had fabulous parents, and there was nothing for me or my parents to fear. It was years and years later that one of these girl friends and I were discussing pornography and she said her first exposure was at one of these sleep-overs.

I said, "Where was I?"

She said, "You always went home early. It happened later in the night."

I said, "Which of the girls brought the pornography?"

She said, "None of them. It was the friend of the brother."

Thankfully, I dodged that bullet. But if I had not been so lucky or confident, I might have felt more comfortable calling my parents and saying quietly, "Elvis lives," then hanging up the phone.

All kids need an out sometimes. Do not think they are one hundred percent safe in this world, despite your best efforts and their best efforts. I was fortunate enough to never get myself into one of these more dangerous situations, but the statistics are that one in five girls is raped and usually by someone they know. I look back on my own life and thank the Lord above for protecting me because, only now as an adult, do I see the potential dangers in some of the choices I made. I was trying hard to make good choices to do what was right and so were my parents. In looking back, I think, *That was so stupid of me to go with that person. That really could have gone south. And oh, that's what was really going on at that party.*

I pray every day for the safety and protection of my children as well as for myself, because looking back, I have proven to be quite stupid and naive. But I also pray that my children will always, always feel that they can come to their parents.

And going back to Reba's song titled, "What Do You Say," what do you say when you pick your kid up from a party gone bad?

> So what do you say in a moment like this
> When you can't find the words to tell it like it is
> Just bite your tongue and let your heart lead the way
> Let's get out of here
> Oh what do you say
> Sometimes you gotta listen to the silence
> And give yourself a little time to think.

Actions always, always, always speak louder than words and rescuing a child with no strings attached is love on top of love. A long hug and kiss on the forehead, a "thank you for being brave enough to call—I will always come," and a shared ice cream might be enough said. Unless it becomes a pattern and then we might need to have an entirely different conversation.

13

HELP FOR COLLEGE

College is expensive. No matter where you go, no matter what you major in, no matter what, it is going to cost a fortune. Now multiply a fortune by the number of kids that you have.

To make this conversation easy and not break the retirement bank, I suggest picking a favorite child or whichever kid has the greatest potential and sending that one kid to college. I'm totally kidding.

My very responsible husband puts a sum of money into each of our kids' college accounts on their birthday. That's great, but it is quite possible that the money we save will never be enough. Consider paying tuition, maybe out of state fees, car insurance, books, apartment, food, gas, maybe living expenses—and multiply that times however many kids you have. It is overwhelming! And who has that kind of money? You might think, "Well, my kids are spread out and only one or two will go at a time."

Don't count those chickens before they hatch. My siblings and I were spread out over ten years, so four kids in ten years. No way we would all end up in college at the same time. I don't know if my parents just weren't living right or what, but four kids in college at the same time happened to them. I'm the oldest and stayed in college late by going to graduate school while my baby brother was invited to go to college after his sophomore year of high school. The two middle children were also in college. My poor parents. How could they possibly help four kids and not sink their own financial ship?

These are the aspects of a college education that we need to discuss, together as parents, far in advance and let our children know so they too can plan accordingly for their own success. The ways in which my parents helped us actually took little to no money.

To help get all of their kids through college, my parents followed a few important steps.

First, they encouraged us to get scholarships. They went so far as to exploit our talents to the right people. I played sports and my Mom helped me build a resume of awards, statistics, pictures, and newspaper clipping, and she made copies. We mailed these to many coaches and schools to bring my accomplishments to their attention, allowing me to get opportunities to try and walk-on at several different schools. You can do this with any talent your child has developed: violin, voice, piano, band, debate, sports, ROTC,

FFA, etc. I earned a full ride scholarship to a junior college and my sister easily could have done the same. There are also the obvious academic scholarships that can be most helpful too. But remember, these often need to be applied for by your child's junior year of high school, so plan ahead, way ahead.

Second, no way could my parents pay for tuition. They encouraged us to get jobs, which we all did. Everyone had one to four part-time jobs *each* while we were attending college. Sometimes this meant we took fewer classes, sometimes it meant we took a semester off to earn money for the next semester.

Finally, my parents also offered some very, very helpful financing. They said, "One way we can help you pay for college is: as long as you are working and going to college, you can live in our house, eat our food, enjoy our electricity, sleep under our roof, use our computers and internet, and keep the cost of college down." Granted, we lived in a town that had a college. But with online courses being available now, the possibilities open up, no matter what town you live in.

The important thing here is that you have a plan before your child walks across the stage and receives that high school diploma. Maybe you say, "I'll pay X number of dollars toward your tuition as long as you maintain a GPA of ___________ and that is good for X number of years. Anything more than that, you will need to take out loans for."

That way maybe your child works for scholarships to make up the difference if the college of their dreams is very expensive. Or maybe they choose the local college because your contribution covers more there. It also gives a deadline for finishing.

There are so many ways to help your child get a higher education, and my purpose in writing this is not to explore all those possibilities but to encourage you to have a plan and communicate that plan to your child. You can always supplement the plan, pay car insurance occasionally, hand them a one-hundred-dollar bill, or pay for books for a semester.

One more thought: not every kid is cut out for college. A good vocational school is perfectly acceptable. No matter how educated you are or hope your children to be, we are not all cut from academic cloth, and thank goodness. Where would we be without our electrician, stone mason, car mechanic, refrigeration guy, welder, or plumber? Some of us would be up a chocolate-colored creek without a paddle, literally.

We want our children to be able to provide for themselves and their families. There are many respectable trades that can do this. In the 1990s book *The Millionaire Next Door*, they reported that the number one "millionaire next door" profession was an auto mechanic. If you do not have a college-minded kiddo, think trade school. You might say, "If you do not want to go to college, that is fine, but let's look into a trade school or the military so you can provide for your children someday."

And there is not one single thing wrong with women doing these jobs either. If your little girl wants to cut hair or weld together a fence, go for it. My hairdresser charges me a fortune. The important thing is to graduate and get skills, whether it is in a formal classroom or in a hands-on situation.

Have a plan, tell your child, and encourage them to choose wisely. God willing and the creek don't rise: they will get a college degree and you will get to retire someday.

14

THIS IS FOR THE GIRLS

I am going to assume for a minute that you are encouraging your boys to do as we just discussed, finding ways to be happy and productive citizens that also allows them to support a wife and children comfortably—comfortably, not extravagantly. If you are doing this, Excellent! Way to go! If you are not doing this with your sons, stay away from my daughters!

I grew up in a house where my Mother was a "stay-at-home" Mom. It was one of the greatest blessings of my life. (Thanks Mom for doing it; and thanks Dad for supporting her in it. Now that I'm all grown up, I see the wisdom and I also see the sacrifices made while making this lifestyle work. Love you guys.)

For your baby girls, please educate them not only academically and with skills, but help them to understand that most women will at some time in their life be the soul breadwinner in their home. This can happen through a life of being single, through the death or illness of a spouse, through job loss, through disability or divorce. Our daughters need an insurance policy via education and skills so that they can raise your grandbabies no matter what!

Long before cell phones, I remember my Mom being stressed out to the point of tears when my Father would come home hours late from work. (Bless my Father, he was/is a workaholic and the sweetest man you could ever know, but he was not/is not a fabulous communicator and often left the office late, got tied up in traffic, and never called Mom to let her know.) It drove my Mom bananas because she felt like if anything ever happened to Dad she could not properly support their four young kids. I remember her telling my sister and me, "You will get your education. You will go to college. If something happened to your Father, I don't know what I would do. You have to have a backup plan."

My Mom was so right. No one wants their daughter to be stuck in a bad situation. And look at the good character and confidence building these life skills can have. One of my best friends put her husband through medical school. She had her own hair salon and was a Mom to her little girls all while her husband was able to focus on becoming a doctor. Today few people would ever guess that my dear friend was the primary breadwinner of her home for many years. Now her spouse does the breadwinning, but if something ever happened to him, she has the confidence, grit, and skill to know that she would be okay.

I have friends who have parted with their spouses either temporarily or permanently and thank the good Lord that they were able to use their education and skills to support their children. We all know circumstances that were not so happy and the ending became overwhelming and even devastating because poverty was either deepened or introduced.

Please, please, please educate your girls. When our country (yes, the US government) wants to change a culture of a people, what do they do? They open schools for the girls. They teach them to read and write and think for themselves. Even our government, with all its flaws and hangups, understands that to change a society—to redefine a culture for the better—is done through educating women.

An African proverb says, "If you educate a man, you educate an individual. If you educate a woman, you educate a family (nation)."

Summing it up, this book is in no way inclusive of all the important chats you should have with your children as they are growing up. But I hope you feel encouraged to be proactive and help your children plan for their futures. Keep communications open and all expectations on the table so your children can see them and know where the lines are in the sand.

If your child wants to live at home after high school graduation, tell them ahead of time, "You can live here on these terms for X amount of time and if you are meeting these conditions."

If you have financial means, explain to your children what you believe about money. Will they inherit it? Will they inherit it with terms? Are you going to will it to charity? This is a growing trend right now among some of the wealthiest people in the world.

If your child and their spouse fall on hard times, is living with you an option? There is no right or wrong answer, but you must communicate the terms long before the moving truck arrives. And just a suggestion, I'm going to go out on a limb and say it is a lot easier to lay this one down without a daughter-in-law or son-in-law already in the picture. So have this conversation with your children long before there is a wedding.

No one can write an all-inclusive book on these conversations because our lives and children are so different and you're going to run into situations that are completely off your grid and mine. The moral of the story is plan ahead, communicate then communicate some more, follow through, teach your kids to think for themselves and accept responsibility. Pray hard and often. There is no sure fire formula for successful parenting, but these things helped my parents be four for four. May you fight like a ninja warrior for your principles, and "may the force be with you."

BIBLIOGRAPHY

42 The True Story of an American Legend. Directed by Brian Helgeland. Performed by Chadwick Boseman, Harrison Ford, Nicole Beharie. Warner Brothers, 2013. DVD.

McEntire, Reba. *What Do You Say?* Reba McIntire. Recorded September 14, 1999. David Malloy, Reba McEntire, 1999, CD.

National Sexual Violence Resource Center. "Statistics About Sexual Violence." 2015. Accessed April 21, 2016. www.nsvrc.org/sites/default/files/publications_ nsvrc_factsheet_media-packet_statistics-about-sexual-violence_0.pdf.

Ondrasik, John. *100 Years.* Five for Fighting. Gregg Wattenberg, 2003, CD.

Stanley, Thomas J., and William D. Danko. *The Millionaire next Door: The Surprising Secrets of America's Wealthy.* Atlanta, GA: Longstreet Press, 1996.

Star Wars. Directed by George Lucas. Performed by Harrison Ford. Los Angeles, CA: Lucasfulm, 1977. DVD.

The Church of Jesus Christ of Latter-day Saints. "The Family: A Proclamation to the World." News release, September 23, 1995. Accessed April 22, 2016. https://www.lds.org/topics/family-proclamation?lang=eng.

Wright, Greg. *Daddy Dates: Four Daughters, One Clueless Dad, and His Quest to Win Their Hearts*. Nashville, TN: Thomas Nelson, 2011.

Made in the USA
San Bernardino, CA
11 August 2016